Moses
CROSSES THE RED SEA

Published in Nashville, Tennessee, by Tommy Nelson™,
a division of Thomas Nelson, Inc.
Managing Editor: Laura Minchew
Project Manager: Karen Gallini
Editor: Tama Fortner

Designed by Koechel Peterson & Associates
Digital color enhancement by Carolyn Guske
Cover illustration by Nathan Fowkes

Library of Congress Cataloging-in-Publication Data

Simon, Mary Manz, 1948–
    Moses crosses the Red Sea : a story of faith and courage / by Mary Manz Simon.
       p.   cm. — (The Prince of Egypt values series)
    Summary: Even in the face of Pharaoh's anger and the pursuit of the Egyptian
soldiers, Moses courageously leads the Israelites out of Egypt.
    ISBN 0-8499-5852-0
    1. Moses (Biblical leader)—Juvenile literature. [1. Moses (Biblical leader) 2. Bible
stories—O.T. 3. Courage.] I. Title. II. Series: Simon, Mary Manz, 1948– Prince of
Egypt values series.
BS580.M6S486   1998
222′.1209505—dc21
                                                          98-38568
                                                          CIP
                                                          AC

Printed in the United States of America

98 99 00 01 02 03 QPH 9 8 7 6 5 4 3 2 1

THE PRINCE OF EGYPT

Timeless Values COLLECTION

Moses
CROSSES THE RED SEA
A Story of Faith and Courage

by MARY MANZ SIMON

tommy
NELSON

Thomas Nelson, Inc.
Nashville

"*I* said *hurry*!" shouted an Egyptian guard, cracking his whip at an old man struggling to lift a large block of stone.

All around, as far as the eye could see, thousands of Hebrew men, women, and children toiled in the hot desert sun, the sting of the overseers' whips on their backs. They were slaves of Pharaoh, the supreme ruler of Egypt. Brick by brick and block by heavy stone block, the Hebrews worked to build the temples and monuments for Pharaoh.

$\mathcal{B}$ut the Hebrew people were God's people. They cried out to God to rescue them. So God chose Moses, a Hebrew who had grown up as a prince of Egypt, to deliver them. This is the story of how Moses, a man of faith and courage, led the Hebrew people out of the land of Egypt.

"Let my people go!" Moses said to Pharaoh as he stood on the banks of the river Nile.

But Pharaoh refused and sent his guards to capture Moses. As the guards came closer, Moses looked at his staff and remembered God's words at the burning bush: "With this staff, you shall do My wonders."

Moses' heart filled with courage, and he touched the river with his staff. The entire river turned to blood!

The guards turned and ran away from Moses. But still Pharaoh would not let the Hebrews go!

So God sent more punishments down on Pharaoh and his people. Millions of frogs hopped through the streets and into homes. Swarms of insects buzzed everywhere. Darkness covered Egypt for three days. Pharaoh became angrier and angrier. God gave Moses the courage to go to Pharaoh again and again, but Pharaoh still would not let the Hebrews go.

Then God sent the tenth punishment, and it was the worst of all. As weeping filled all of Egypt, Pharaoh sent for Moses and said, "You and your people have my permission to go."

Moses hurried from the palace. The Hebrews must leave quickly, before Pharaoh changed his mind.

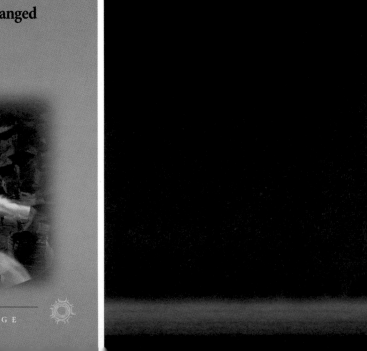

"**W**e're free! We're free! We're finally free!" The message flew from house to house.

God's people scurried through the darkness, gathering what they would need for the journey ahead.

Tired children were awakened from their sleep. Men calmed animals, startled to be led outside at the unusual hour. Women threw unbaked breads into pans. Clothing was quickly packed. The sounds of braying donkeys and clanking harnesses filled the night.

$\mathcal{M}$oses, once a prince of Egypt but now the deliverer of God's people, led growing numbers of Hebrew people through the winding streets. At last, they reached the gates of Egypt—then went through them to freedom. The people wound their way through the desert, down valleys, and around hills. At last they came to the Red Sea. But as the people were resting, an unmistakable sound echoed through the camp. An Egyptian horn! With each blast of the horn, the people grew more afraid.

The Hebrews heard the thundering of horses and chariots before they saw the army. But soon six hundred Egyptian chariots stretched across the entire crest of a distant mountain.

Fearful that they would soon be killed by Pharaoh's soldiers, the Hebrew people lost all their courage. They turned to Moses and shouted:

"We're trapped here!"

"How can we escape?"

"What do we do now?"

As Moses looked from the Hebrew people to the Egyptian chariots and then to the Red Sea, his courage sank. He walked to the edge of the sea, looked at the staff in his hand, and then up to heaven. Once again, he remembered God's words, "With this staff, you shall do My wonders." With new courage, Moses turned to the Hebrews and said, "Do not be afraid. God will fight for you."

And so, God's miracle began. The Hebrew people drew back in amazement, as the water surged and parted. A pathway appeared between two towering walls of water. Clutching their belongings, the Hebrews hurried down into the sea.

Walls of water towered far above them,
and the Hebrews stared at the sea
creatures that swam by next to them.
At last, the Hebrews scrambled up the
banks of the other shore—just in time.

Clouds of dust signaled the arrival of

the Egyptian soldiers at the water's edge.

The army paused, but Pharaoh ordered

his soldiers to keep following the

Hebrews. So Pharaoh's finest soldiers

charged into the parted waters.

*I*mmediately God threw the Egyptians into confusion.

Horses reared up. Armor broke. Soldiers toppled.

Harnesses and chariots fell in tangled heaps. Still

the soldiers rushed onward.

"The soldiers! They're coming!" cried Moses. But

God saw the soldiers and sent the walls of water

crashing down on top of them. The waters covered

the entire Egyptian army.

The Hebrew people were saved! They sang praises to God, knowing that God had sent the courageous Moses to lead them to freedom. Having seen all of God's miracles, the Hebrews now felt new courage in their hearts as they looked forward to the journey to the Promised Land.

To Think About

Courage means doing what you know is right. It is not always easy to show courage, though. It was not easy for Moses to tell Pharaoh to let the Hebrew people go. Moses knew that Pharaoh was a very powerful ruler. He could have had Moses thrown in jail or worse! But Moses knew that facing Pharaoh was the right thing to do. Moses also knew that God would give him the courage he needed, because he was doing the right thing. And so, the Hebrew people were freed.

There will be times when you will need to show courage—when you will need to do what you know is right. For example, someone might ask you to do something wrong. He or she might ask you to steal something, to lie to your parents, to cheat on a test, or even to try drugs! Sometimes people will say things like, "I won't be your friend if you don't do this." But you know these things are wrong, and a true friend would not ask you to do them. Ask God for courage, then do what you know is right. Then you, too, will be a person of courage—just like Moses.

To Talk About

1. Why did Moses ask Pharaoh to let God's people leave Egypt?

2. Why did Moses need courage to face Pharaoh?

3. Courage comes from knowing we can count on God. What was one way God helped Moses?

4. Having courage doesn't always mean leading thousands of people to freedom. When have you asked God for courage?

5. When have you seen another person do what was right, even though it was hard or scary?

6. How did Moses give courage to the Hebrews when they were trapped at the Red Sea?

7. The Hebrew people needed courage to begin their journey to the Promised Land. When have you needed courage in a new situation?

8. What other Bible heroes showed courage?